ELEMENTAL

FIONA BARRATT-CAMPBELL

ELEMENTAL

Written by Fiona Barratt-Campbell
Foreword by Tony Chambers
Interiors Photography by Ray Main
Portrait Photography by Chris Floyd

RIZZOLI
NEW YORK
New York · Paris · London · Milan

CONTENTS

FOREWORD

I distinctly remember first meeting Fiona Barratt-Campbell. It was February 2013 and at the suggestion of a mutual friend, Marie Moatti, who was certain we'd get on. Marie is a brilliant creative matchmaker, so she arranged a "casual" dinner for six (including our respective partners) at The Arts Club on Dover Street.

Marie was right—Fiona is one of those people who makes an instant, positive impression, and that impression lasts. Her passion for her design work and her business is infectious, and she communicates it with such clarity and sincerity that you leave feeling upbeat and stimulated.

At that time, Fiona's interior design business was well established and flourishing, with the studio working on some of the finest high-end residential and commercial spaces. But, always the entrepreneur, Fiona was also in the process of launching a new venture—her eponymous furniture and product brand, FBC London.

It was this exciting venture that sparked my imagination and set off a memorable collaboration for *Wallpaper** magazine's legendary Handmade project—an annual exhibition of creativity and craftsmanship at Salone del Mobile in Milan.

Fiona's contribution, a cast-bronze sculptural valet, designed in collaboration with luxury fashion house Alexander McQueen, was a showstopper—encapsulating her full repertoire of skills. Combining contemporary aesthetics with traditional craftsmanship and innovative thinking, it comprised an array of added goodies: a tray for gadgets, a pullout tie and belt holder, a shoehorn, a shoe stand, and USB-charging ports. It also promoted the best in British manufacturing techniques with companies such as Powderhall Bronze Foundry carrying out the lost-wax casting, and Nicklin Furniture producing the hand carving and engraving.

A year or so later Fiona made another bold move and introduced her studio and showroom space in London's Victoria neighborhood. An exquisite renovation of a former post office building, the 6,500-square-foot gallery-style space provided a chic industrial backdrop for the brand's opulent designs. It also allowed her to showcase the work of other designers/makers she admired—such as American rising stars Lindsey Adelman and Studio Apparatus—illustrating her keen eye for talent-spotting and her retail sense.

We've stayed in touch continually since then, both in a social and a work capacity, and I never cease to be amazed by her skillful and effortless capacity (well it appears effortless) to juggle her creative and business commitments with her family and social obligations. And I'm thrilled to see this timely, much-deserved publication documenting her work so far. It's a testament to her passionate creativity, prodigious work ethic, and business acumen, all of which were so evident at our first meeting. I feel these three attributes are the key ingredients to Fiona's success and should be a guidance for any aspiring young designer. They are, dare I say, elemental.

Tony Chambers
Founder and Creative Director of Studio TC & Friends.
Creative Director and Editor-in-Chief of Wallpaper* *from 2003 –2018*

INTRODUCTION

Fiona Barratt-Campbell

I decided to call this book *Elemental* because it expresses something fundamental in my approach to design. Whether it's the homes and hospitality spaces I create for clients around the globe or the products I develop for FBC London, I have become known for an aesthetic that is timeless and powerful, for using natural materials and finishes that have a solid, permanent quality.

Growing up in the northeast of England was invaluable in shaping my character. I was fortunate to enjoy the freedom of roaming the rugged Northumberland hills and the miles of white-sand beaches with the powerful crashing waves of the cold North Sea. This raw and unrefined landscape ignited my passion for the beauty that nature creates and with this the hugely diverse inspiration it provides. Nature along with travel is my primary source of inspiration for both interior and furniture designs. The constant evolution of nature provides an ever-changing plethora of textures, colors, and shapes that can be interpreted into many forms of design. Today our studio is known for the unique use of texture within our designs.

It was my admiration for the ancient Romans that first drew me to strong natural materials like wood, metal, and stone—and yet I believe it's important to counterbalance their solid, elemental qualities with soft and tactile finishes, to add a sense of warmth and comfort. For me, the layering of different textures is the cornerstone of graceful design.

After completing high school, I moved from the northeast to London to study interior and spatial design at Chelsea College of Arts, which is part of the University of the Arts London. I took a year off to continue my interior design studies at Parsons School of Design in New York. What was so wonderful about having the opportunity to study at both of these prestigious institutions is that they follow such different schools of thought. Chelsea College is very conceptual in its teaching and curriculum, whereas Parsons was practical and progressive in preparing students for the workplace.

The entrepreneurial gene runs strong in my family. My grandfather, Sir Lawrence Barratt, the founder of Barratt Developments, was a well-known and respected businessman in the UK. He was the pioneer of making new homes affordable to all. He was an extremely astute and driven man. My parents, Peter and Angela, were also successful in their chain of retail garden centers that they founded and built together for twenty-seven years before selling it. I always admired them for working together. This is something that my husband, Sol, and I have been fortunate to do with our furniture brand, FBC London. It is invaluable to have a completely unbiased and truthful voice. In the design industry especially, this is crucial. Design is about evolution and benefits wholly from critical appreciation. Growing up in an entrepreneurial family, I truly understand the hard work and dedication that goes into starting up and running a business, so I was under no illusions of what lay ahead when the time arose for me to start my businesses.

After college I began my career working for a well-known residential interior design firm in London. After three years there I decided it was the right time for me to branch out on my own. In 2006, Fiona Barratt Interiors was formed. Since then we have grown into a well-regarded international studio with a strong design ethic. I have a talented and creative team of individuals who work with me. We have strong principles and ethics, and I believe a successful interior will only derive from a solid and trustworthy relationship with the client. We must understand and interpret each client's vision impeccably.

Texture is the key element in every space I design. I don't use a lot of color or pattern: my signature look tends to be quite tonal, a subtle blend of complementary shades designed to evoke a sense of elegance and depth. Visual interest, warmth, and character are provided by the textures and finishes I layer within each space, into which I then add carefully curated antiques and artworks to provide contrasting accents and pops of color. This, to me, is the essence of the modern luxury aesthetic.

Since launching my interior design company, Fiona Barratt Interiors, the business has grown incrementally. Starting from our very first commission—a 12,000-square-foot ski chalet in Verbier, Switzerland, for Richard Branson—we have continued to extend the scope of our work, with an ever-expanding portfolio that now comprises a mix of exquisite private homes and hotel projects in the UK and abroad, in locations such as Mallorca, Hong Kong, Moscow, and Beirut.

One of the most wonderful aspects of my profession is having the privilege of meeting such a diverse demographic of people of different ages and from different cultures and countries. The enrichment it brings to me and a project is invaluable. I particularly enjoy life stories and hearing about the places/situations that people have experienced. It is vital in gaining a real understanding of clients and how they envisage their home.

In 2013 we launched FBC London, our furniture brand. More recently, we added bespoke kitchens to this brand. These pieces are predominantly inspired by nature and Roman architecture and artifacts. I wanted to design pieces that were a real part of my heritage, creating antiques for the future. New furniture, but with a provenance and a story behind it. Again, as with the interiors, the main focus is texture; for example, high-gloss veneer, cast bronze, sand-blasted woods, brass, and copper, as well as many textured metal patinas combined together.

I am committed to using the world's most talented craftspeople to bring these products to fruition. When we launched our first collection, all of our products were made in the northeast of England, and I'm immensely proud to say that many of our products are still manufactured within a few miles of where I grew up. I also believe it is important to include a local element in every interior design project I take on—whether it's utilizing sand from a nearby beach to make plaster for the walls of a coastal villa in Mallorca or fabricating a bespoke dining table from disused railway ties for a Georgian country house in Yorkshire.

Expert craftsmanship and the melding of traditional and modern techniques are at the core of everything we do at FBC London. We don't follow fashion; our goal is simply to make things that we love, using the rarest and finest materials available. This, in essence, is what makes a design successful: attention to detail; integrity; never compromising on quality; and the fact that every aspect of every piece we produce has been extensively considered, reworked, and refined.

PROJECTS

HISTORIC TOWN HOUSE

LONDON, UK

This is my home and invariably the most difficult project for me to design; however, the advantage of having lived in our home prior to the refurbishment was invaluable in determining the spatial planning.

Our home is situated on the banks of the river Thames in Chelsea and overlooks Battersea Park. The importance of flowing water in front of our property is key to a good movement of energy. It is a historic Georgian home built on the site of King Henry VIII's old manor house, giving way to a vibrant history underneath our foundations. The aspect from the front is the spectacular Albert Bridge, magically twinkling with thousands of lights every evening. Neighboring gardens merge with ours to create an oasis of calm in the center of London. The most beautiful magnolia trees fill the air with a heavenly scent when in bloom.

When we first bought this property, it was just my husband and me, so we very much designed this for a couple. Now, ten years later with three children and a dog to consider, we recently renovated the house again by making substantial changes that suit family life while maintaining original period features of the property. We were careful to maintain the elegant Georgian heritage that is woven through the fabric of this house by considered development of new spaces and the preservation of existing heritage details; for example, the beautiful delicate cornicing and traditional wood paneling to the ground-floor morning room and the first-floor living room. In both these rooms we added a softness to the paneling by insetting it with leather and silk in the living room. The treatment of walls is hugely important to the feel of the space, and within our home I have curated a vast mix of textures with the wall coverings: traditional silk, leather panels, oxidized copper sheets, cork tiles, specialist plaster, rolled hand-painted porcelain, hemp cloth, and textured gold leaf.

The rooms throughout our home are a classic example of my design philosophies: layered textures and strong, clean statement pieces of contemporary furniture and lighting reside seamlessly alongside antique and artisanal pieces. We have spent many years sourcing and curating these pieces of furniture and art from all over the world, providing a real reflection of our characters.

What is so wonderful about furniture is how you can give it new life when you move or relocate it to a different room within your home and place it alongside different colors and pieces. There are several pieces of furniture and lighting in our home that have been moved numerous times until I feel the evolutionary process of curated design has been completed.

KELLY WEARSTLER

KELLY WEARSTLER
COSMOPOLITAN LIVING

BLAUPUNKT
LW
MW
SW
SOLO

HISTORIC HALL

YORKSHIRE, UK

This historic Georgian country house, situated in the wonderfully scenic Yorkshire Dales, was originally built and inhabited by monks. It required extensive building works to make it habitable for a family. Architecturally it was an interesting project, as the main historic hall and the four-hundred-year-old barns had to be connected. This was done with a contrasting modern extension to the existing buildings. The juxtaposition of the clean architectural modern addition against the existing stone-built Georgian hall is surprisingly seamless, and the new addition now adds a layer of modern interest to the property.

One of the main challenges with this project was to fulfill the mandate to make this a family home. The sheer scale of the project was enormous (24,000 square feet) with the mix of architectural building styles and varying room sizes, not only in footprint but ceiling heights, which ranged from about 6 ½ feet to 30 feet. Success depended on the seamless connectivity of the spaces. As you pass through the property, the journey is one of exploration and a feast for the senses. The walk down the long corridor in the two-hundred-fifty-year-old hall toward a small single door at the end gives way to the monolithic kitchen and dining room: 2,500 square feet in size with 30-foot ceilings. The ceiling features an exposed steel framework; the floor is polished concrete. We designed a mezzanine to float across the vast void. It is simplistic in its design and materials (glass and wood) to complement the pared-back and robust materiality of the other finishes within this space. The general palette throughout is subtle. Natural muted beiges and grays tone into the earthy palette that is present from every window.

We designed several custom tables that were constructed using one-hundred-year-old reclaimed railway ties that came from the Yorkshire railways. We used a local artisan to make these for us. I feel that it is important to embrace the locality of a building, adding relevance and provenance by incorporating local materials with a story.

Lighting, although extremely important in all projects, was a major feature throughout this property. It is absolutely key to design the lighting to complement spaces and features without overpowering the content. At night the transformation of the internal and external spaces can only be described as magical and almost theatrical.

CHANDON

LA MAISON DE VERRE
5 BEDMaR & SHi

ABOVE PARIS
MOROCCO
TOM FORD

Morocco
MOROCCO
TOM
TOM FORD

HISTORIC HALL

NORTHUMBERLAND, UK

Set in the wonderfully rugged landscape of the Northumberland hills, this historic Georgian country house (the first unfortified property to be built in Northumberland) has been our family retreat from the chaos of London. Over several years we undertook extensive renovations to the main hall, cottages, outbuildings, and formal gardens. The house is situated in what was "no man's land"—the land to the north where the Romans made the boundary of their empire, Hadrian's Wall. Stone was taken from the wall nearly three hundred years ago and used in the construction of the house. "Hallington Hall" in ancient Celtic means holy valley, and it is very much a sanctuary of calm, which is ironic given the bloody history of the land on which the house resides.

When you own a property of this age and history, we believe you become a custodian for the future, and you must restore with integrity, quality, and passion. These houses have stood for many years and will stand for centuries to come.

As always with a historic building, the main challenges arise when trying to integrate modern mechanical, electrical, and technological requirements within existing walls and ceiling voids without compromising the existing features. The majority of the changes to the internal layouts came in the introduction of en suite bathrooms on the first and second floors. The property has been fortunate to have only two owners in its history, and it had not been updated in more than fifty years (only one of the nine bedrooms had an en suite bathroom). The rooms are beautifully proportioned both in height and space and afford views across either the romantically wild Northumberland countryside or our beautifully manicured gardens. The period paneling and cornicing was reinstated throughout, along with the introduction of missing period fireplaces.

There are many workshops and talented artisans in the northeast of England. It is important to support these local trades, and where possible, we utilized their skills during the construction and fit-out stages of the build. All of the built-in joinery, including the custom-design kitchen cabinetry and handles, was made locally in a workshop located on the banks of the river Tyne in Newcastle.

AVERY

a life less ordinary
ANDREW MARTIN INTERIOR DESIGN REVIEW
teNeues

230
229

SULZEER

HISTORIC TOWN HOUSE

SOMERSET, UK

This property is located in a historic city in the West Country. It is a fine example of Georgian architecture at its best. Arranged over six floors with a south-facing garden, there was a marginal amount of building work required, as the property had recently been renovated and retained all the original historic features.

The mandate was to create a comfortable family home with a more traditional aesthetic, since the clients wished to incorporate their beautifully curated antique and art collection. It is such a great privilege to work with such historically important artwork and furniture pieces. I personally enjoy the quality that a fine oil painting in a traditional frame brings to an interior. The contrast of modern contemporary pieces with antiques creates a grounded atmosphere, as well as character and belonging. The intricacies of the construction and the detailing on antiques offer a complementary contrast to the simpler and more elegant design of the contemporary furniture.

This project was about the journey of layering with new and old. Having such a large selection of furniture that has been carefully selected by the client over many years brings an added dynamic to the design process. It is very much about understanding the vision and then completing the jigsaw of the design. Before I can embark on the journey of design, it's integral that I understand our clients' vision.

Maximizing the usable internal area is paramount in any property, as space is such a valuable commodity. We converted the utilitarian cellar into a cinema, adding wood paneling to the walls and linen to the beautiful arched ceiling. The small windows, which were an advantage when built to keep sunlight out to protect the food and wine stored there, are now an advantage in a room used to watch movies.

We added to the existing fabric of the building through specialized finishes on the walls and with a varied materiality of fabrics and finishes on the furniture. For example, a textured, sandblasted, blackened-ash wall in the dining room contrasts with the smooth slightly glossy finish of an old oil painting in its ornate gold frame. The large antique chandelier hanging above a contemporary table contrasts with vibrant red leather chairs.

HAM HOUSE

MARTELL
MACALLAN

CITY APARTMENT

MOSCOW, RUSSIA

When I first visited this apartment, it was a blank canvas in the true sense of the word. It was a new-build apartment consisting of a concrete shell with windows. Situated in the center of Moscow, and within close proximity to Red Square and the Bolshoi Theatre, this apartment is nestled in an area of both new and old buildings. It needed to be a sanctuary of calm and relaxation within a busy city. There was a focus on entertaining family and friends as well as an area for music, since several members of the family are keen musicians.

The key for me was to create for the family a home that, although entirely new, felt established. We achieved this with the key principles I abide by. I don't follow fashions, and I believe in creating an interior that feels that it belongs within its four walls and not isolated within its location. This was my first project in Russia. I had been eager to work there for many years, and I was fortunate to have such wonderful clients who placed their entire trust in me and their daughter to create their home.

The local architect and contractor were extremely professional and helped to deliver an exemplary finish. The local craftsmen were meticulous in their finishing.

One of the most interesting aspects of working internationally is having an insight into how trades and industry operate overseas. I relish the opportunity to work with local trades and welcome the talent they can contribute to a project.

The space is arranged over one floor; however, the spatial planning was challenging: the kitchen and bathrooms had to remain in the same position owing to fixed pipework runs, so incorporating the gym and beauty room among other requirements needed extremely concise arrangements.

The apartment showcases the most diverse selection of finishes throughout. This was a conscious decision, as I wanted to bring warmth and character to this new build, especially since Moscow has such a diverse temperature range. I wanted the space to feel open and airy in the summer, yet cozy and comforting during the winter months. The dining room features a vibrant wall of blue resin with a textured silver patina subbase. Visually, it appears like the ocean with a reflective quality—a smooth, gently undulating surface. In the beauty room the wallpaper is made of jute sacking with a painted finish applied over the top. I like the irony of using such a utilitarian material as jute and reinventing it into a luxury product. It also imbues the space with an earthy quality.

The kitchen was one of the first FBC kitchens that I designed from our retail brand. Handcrafted in England, it features high-gloss walnut and gray oak cabinets along with brass detailing and a rare marble worktop. The cabinets above the cooktop have a unique design: an imprint of a cabbage leaf that was cast in resin and coated in bronze patina. These small details bring a sense of character and rarity to a design.

THE PHOTO
MAP
FANTASTIC MAN
PARIS
TURNER

RUSSIA
PAUL CEZANNE
SOMME
GENESIS?
THE CLASSIC CARS BOOK
GENESIS
TASCHEN
THE CENTURY OF MODERN DESIGN
MALT WHISKY

fly

away

away

PIZZA
TASTY!
A HISTORY OF FOOD IN 100 RECIPES
WILLIAM SITWELL

VOGUE ON GIORGIO ARMANI
VOGUE ON RALPH LAUREN
VOGUE ON YVES SAINT LAURENT
VOGUE ON HUBERT DE GIVENCHY

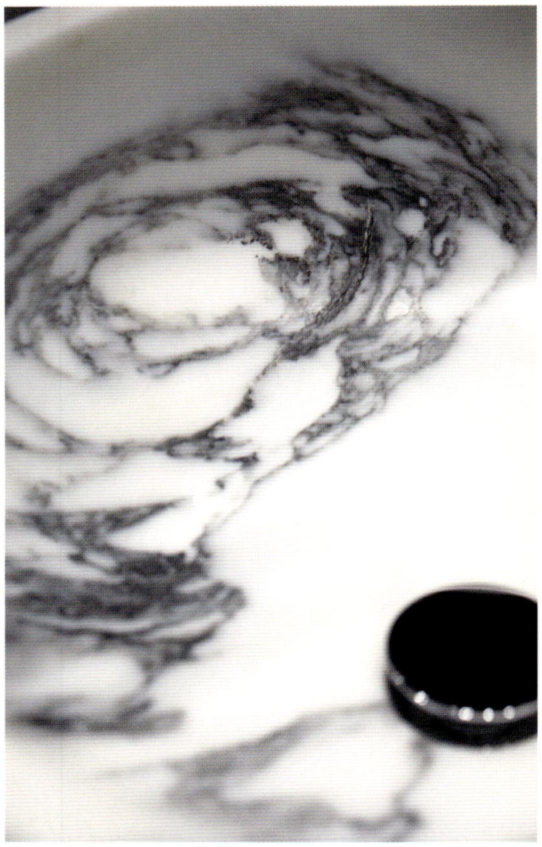

BEACH VILLA
MALLORCA, SPAIN

I have worked with these clients for many years, and this was the second property we designed for them. We are currently working on the fourth commission in over a decade. I have enjoyed the process of interacting so closely with the same family on such a diverse range of projects (two city, one country, and this beach villa). The diversity of the projects, from the type of building and location, brings new challenges within the remit and the design process. What has been very interesting to witness is how our tastes and styles have evolved over the years, both those of the client and my own; as our lives have changed, what we have been exposed to over the years has shaped our aesthetic. We have also built a deep level of trust that is vital when working on something so personal as a family home.

Located on the beautiful island of Mallorca, my clients purchased two adjoining plots of land on a secluded bay with brilliant panoramic views. Working with a local Spanish architect, the mandate was to create a villa that sat perfectly within its surroundings while maintaining privacy but maximizing the spectacular views.

Practicality and functionality were paramount along with maximizing the flow of natural light into the space. Having worked in many different locations around the world with different climates, I have realized that it is key to the success of a design to adapt the materiality to suit the climatic conditions. Also, where climates are at their most diverse, natural materials are always more functional. Here we used a seamless, poured microcement throughout for the floors; the finish resembles the floor of a traditional Spanish finca.

All sanitary ware was brushed stainless steel, as plated hardware will rust with the sea air. We clad feature walls in a combination of wenge and Iroko wood, which have a tight grain and high oil content that are perfect for hot, sea environments. It was also important that all the materials we used wore well with age. All the fabrics—linens, cottons, wools, and leather—were kept as natural as possible and in muted tones. The rugs throughout are also made of natural fibers: hyacinth matting or felt.

A selection of accessories and furniture were sourced locally from antique shops, adding character among the contemporary pieces. The antiques also complement the pared-back architectural detailing throughout.

Lighting, as always, was extremely important. As this property is very much an indoor/outdoor home, the lighting outside needed to be an extension of the interior.

With so many large windows, it was important to consider what was seen through them: What was the vignette looking in at night, as opposed to the view looking out during the day? With this in mind, the decorative lights were the focus, especially in the master bedroom, with the subtle and organic hanging lamps made with handblown glass globes and held together with knotted rope, and in the kitchen, with the custom-designed light over the kitchen island made of steel with simple caged bulb holders.

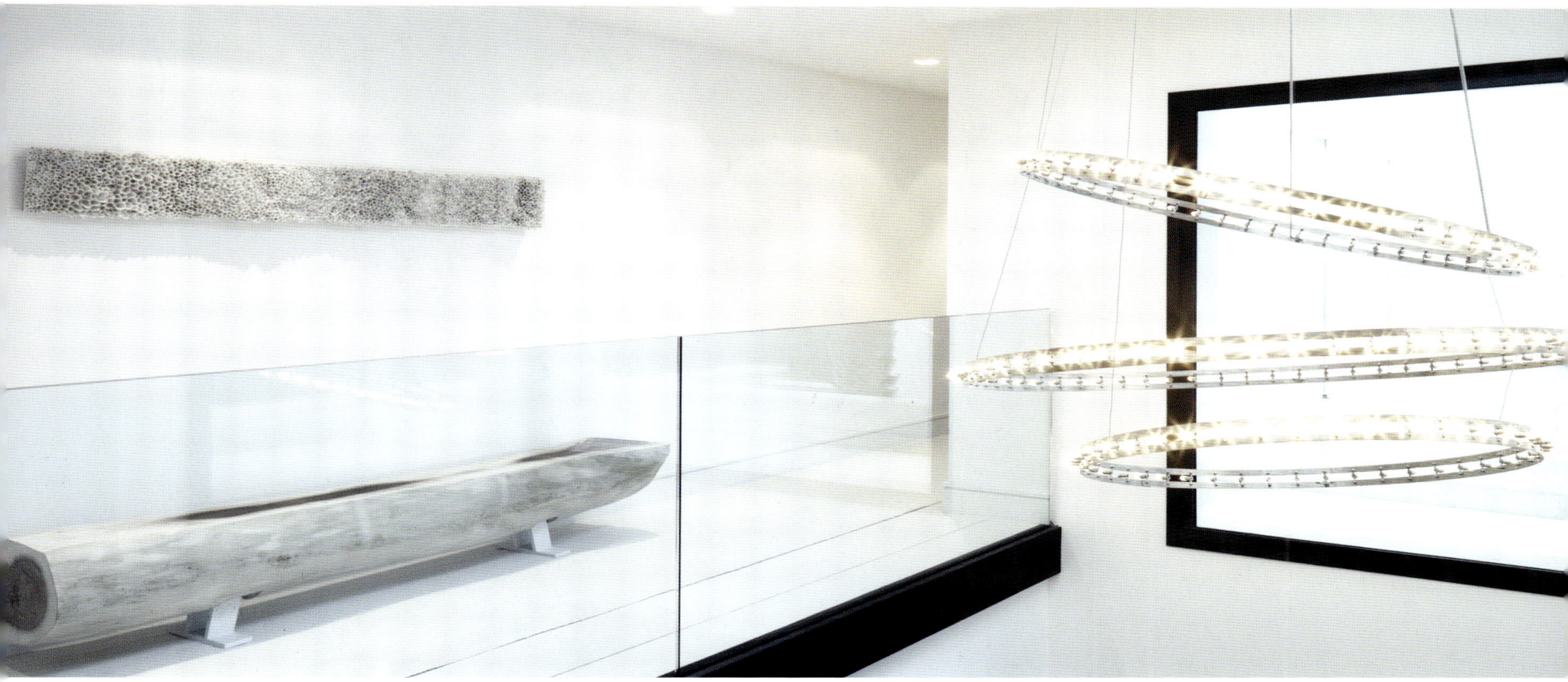

THE SEA

ocean

RIVERSIDE DEVELOPMENT

LONDON, UK

This modern new development is located on the banks of the river Thames. The apartment enjoys spectacular views both east and west along the river. A stone's throw from the Houses of Parliament, it is ideally located for this titled client.

Since this apartment was newly completed, our mandate was to provide a furniture package only. What I specifically enjoyed about this project was the remit to incorporate many of the clients' existing antiques into this modern environment. They also have a vast collection of more than seven hundred paintings; we worked with them to select several for this project. The balancing act of mixing antique and modern is a delicate one, and all the items were carefully considered to achieve a successful outcome: neither too much of one or the other.

As their preferred style is more traditional, I wanted to make sure that we achieved character that complemented the existing modern features. To house all their many ornaments and objets d'art we had to incorporate display shelving. We used a company based in Philadelphia with an industrial style refined for residential use. We added these shelving units—with their beautiful detailing—in the kitchen and the study. The open format is perfect for displaying their collection.

Fabrics were luxurious and more traditional. For the curtains in the living room we used a patterned linen with braiding to the leading edges. We also used silks, silk velvet, and cashmere, among other materials. A pair of antique chairs in the living room were reupholstered in velvet, and we added a long traditional fringe. Three pieces of art were hung at different heights above these chairs, and the grandfather clock was placed at the side. I am particularly fond of this aspect. Setting the antique pieces in an irregular format against the clean wall gives them a new, fresh aesthetic.

CITY APARTMENT

LONDON, UK

Located in the heart of Knightsbridge, London, this new-build triplex apartment extends over three floors: ground, basement, and subbasement. Even though over half of the apartment is subterranean, it doesn't feel like it. The clever spatial planning allows light to filter to all floors through perfectly positioned light wells: one internal and one external. The internal one drops all three floors and features windows that allow light into the rooms. The external light well drops two floors and features a green wall, adding color and life into the interior.

This apartment is not a primary residence, so it was important that it was low-maintenance and practical for a family of five. Also, owing to the central location, it was paramount that the apartment be a haven of peace and calm—a refuge from the bustling city at their doorstep. The general palette in the communal areas and master suite was kept neutral with accents of color; however, we added plenty of color in the children's bedrooms. The master suite is very much an oasis of serenity. The fabrics and finishes are luxurious but subtle in their application. One of the curtains is sheer lace and the other is linen. The lace casts the most beautiful dappled shadow as the light shines through. The bedside tables are from the City collection of our furniture brand. The rustic chipped oak fronts of the bedside drawers add contrast to the silk carpet and textured plaster wall. We wanted to preserve a sense of positive karma, so, where possible, we kept technology out of sight; for example, the television is concealed in a unit finished in white gray walnut and bronze detailing.

In keeping with the existing modern aesthetic, we kept textures subtle and mainly on the furniture. Most of the walls were painted—the perfect backdrop for the clients' modern art collection.

We designed several bespoke joinery units; on the cabinet at the foot of the stairs, the detailing was inspired by the metal casting trays that are used in the bronze-casting process. The external finish is a smooth dark chocolate oak with the internal finish a contrasting vibrant orange.

TOM FORD

ANNIE LEIBOVIT

ST. TROPEZ

TALKING FASHION
ANIMAL
art
A PRIVILEGED LIFE
BE MY GUEST
ART THE WHOLE STORY
INDIGO

WHAAM!
J.A.M.A

DONT
WALK
WALK
J.A.M.A

MAX

HISTORIC APARTMENT

LONDON, UK

Located on the banks of the Thames in Chelsea, this top-floor lateral four-bedroom apartment in a Victorian mansion block affords spectacular views of the river and toward the wonderfully lush Battersea Park. An apartment of this size on a single level is rare in Chelsea, as many of the properties of this proportion are town houses.

This project was a complete strip back to shell and core, and then rebuilding and fitting out, incorporating modern mechanical and electric services. The existing floor plan was typically Victorian. The principal rooms were arranged as the living and dining rooms and situated at the front of the apartment with the best views.

The kitchen, located in the center of the apartment, was extremely small, overlooking an unattractive internal courtyard. The bedrooms, spaced out down the long corridor, shared one bathroom. The main hurdle we encountered was gaining the permissions to alter the general arrangement of the apartment to suit modern-day living. As a general rule, in these purpose-built mansion blocks, every apartment kept the same layout in terms of kitchens and bathrooms stacked on top of one another for ease of drainage and minimizing leaks. To make this apartment workable for a family we wanted to relocate the kitchen to the front and open it up to the living room. It is fascinating to see how living styles have evolved over the centuries and the knock-on effect this has to the way we live in our homes.

The brief was to create a refined, textural, timeless luxury. All the existing period architectural detailing was kept where possible and reinstated as necessary. A smoked oak large-format chevron floor runs throughout. The kitchen was the first FBC London kitchen and very much characterized the ethos of the brand; luxury British-made cabinetry and finishes with the introduction of bespoke handles, specialist cabinetry, and interesting stones. As the kitchen was open-plan and directly connected to the living room, the finishes needed to harmonize and be appropriately balanced in quality and appearance.

Texture was abundant throughout, as nearly all the walls featured a different finish: for example, sandblasted ash, bronze patina, specialist plaster, textured linen, hemp grass, and stone. This gave each space individuality while retaining a cohesive continuity.

PRESTON BAILEY

10 BILLION STEPHEN
Top

SAVON
LIQUIDE

THE MAKING OF

PRIVÉ ARMOUR CHAIR

'Creating this piece was a real journey of exploration and discovery. The final product realised from true craftsmen, creative and skilled at their trades.

Using a variety of production methods from the technically advanced laser CNC machines to the ancient technique of bronze casting. The combination of both intertwined seamlessly to create a piece that represents the evolution of production methods.'

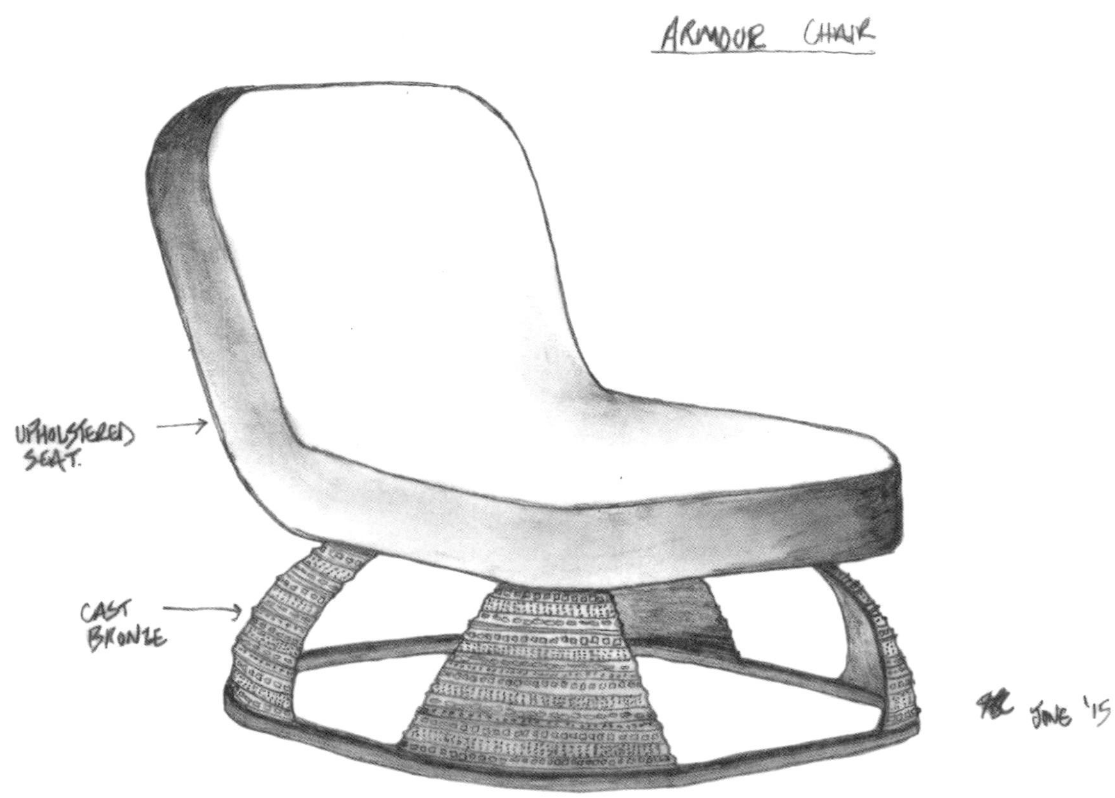

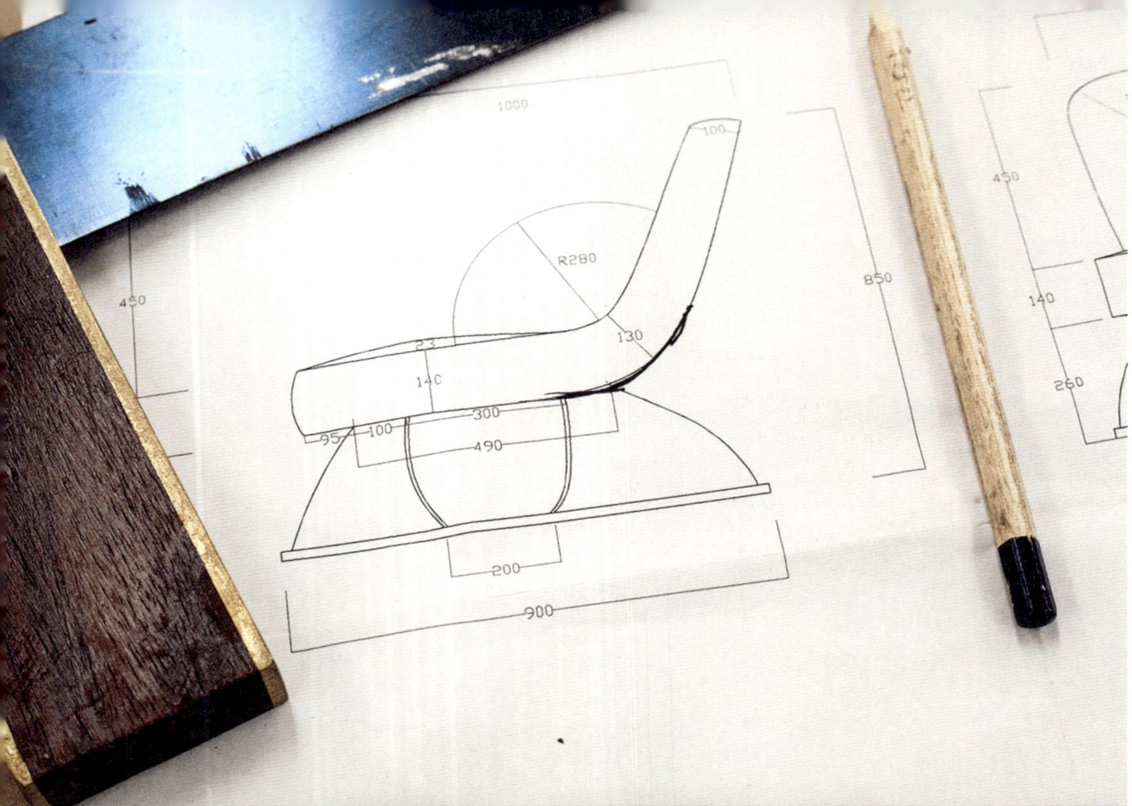
1000
100
R280
130
140
300
490
100
95
450
850
200
900

CARHARTTS

OREGON®
PATENT (BREVET) #5,136,783

PRIVÉ VALET

'I was honoured to be asked to participate in the eponymous Wallpaper Handmade project alongside Alexander McQueen to create a men's valet.
This was a project discovering combinations of materials, functionality verus form, and the melding of ancient and modern production techniques.
It was a lesson about time... The importance of it! Watching the CNC machine carve out the McQueen signature trailing ivy design with absolute precision, pre-programmed, efficient and without error. The hand-carving of the mould for the bronze hanger being the opposite. It's prefection born from trial and error. From, time to review and reassess, giving way to the natural process of evolution.' FBC

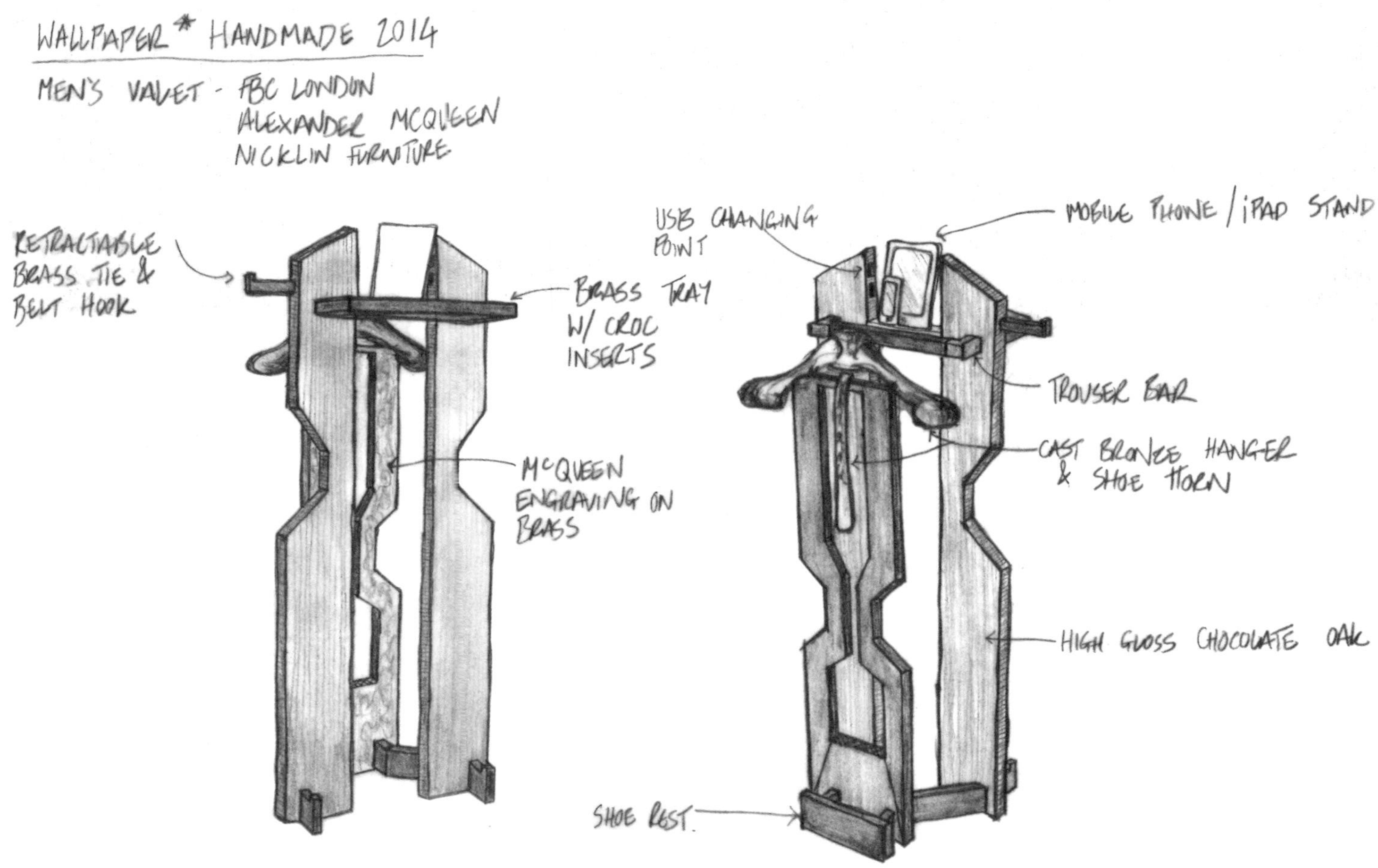

20cm.
45cm

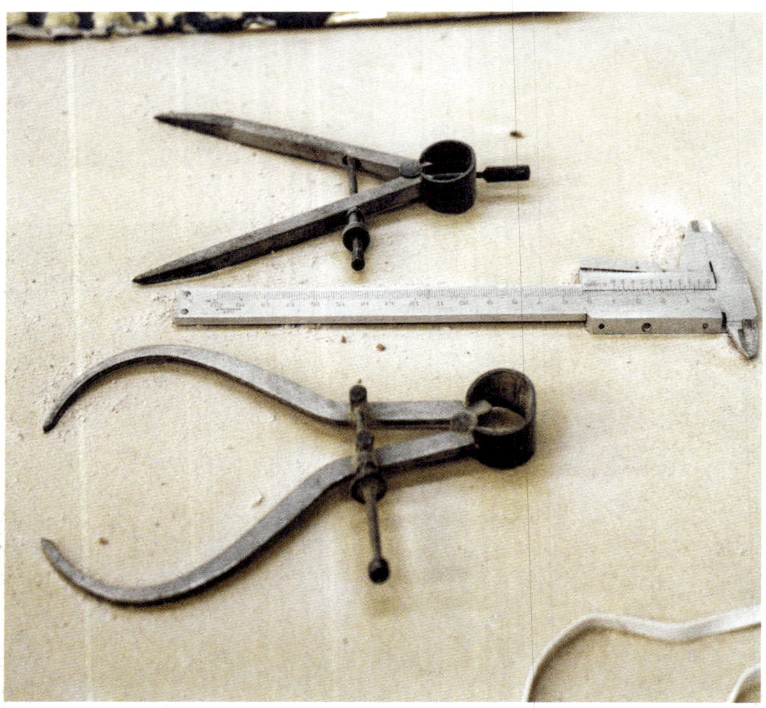

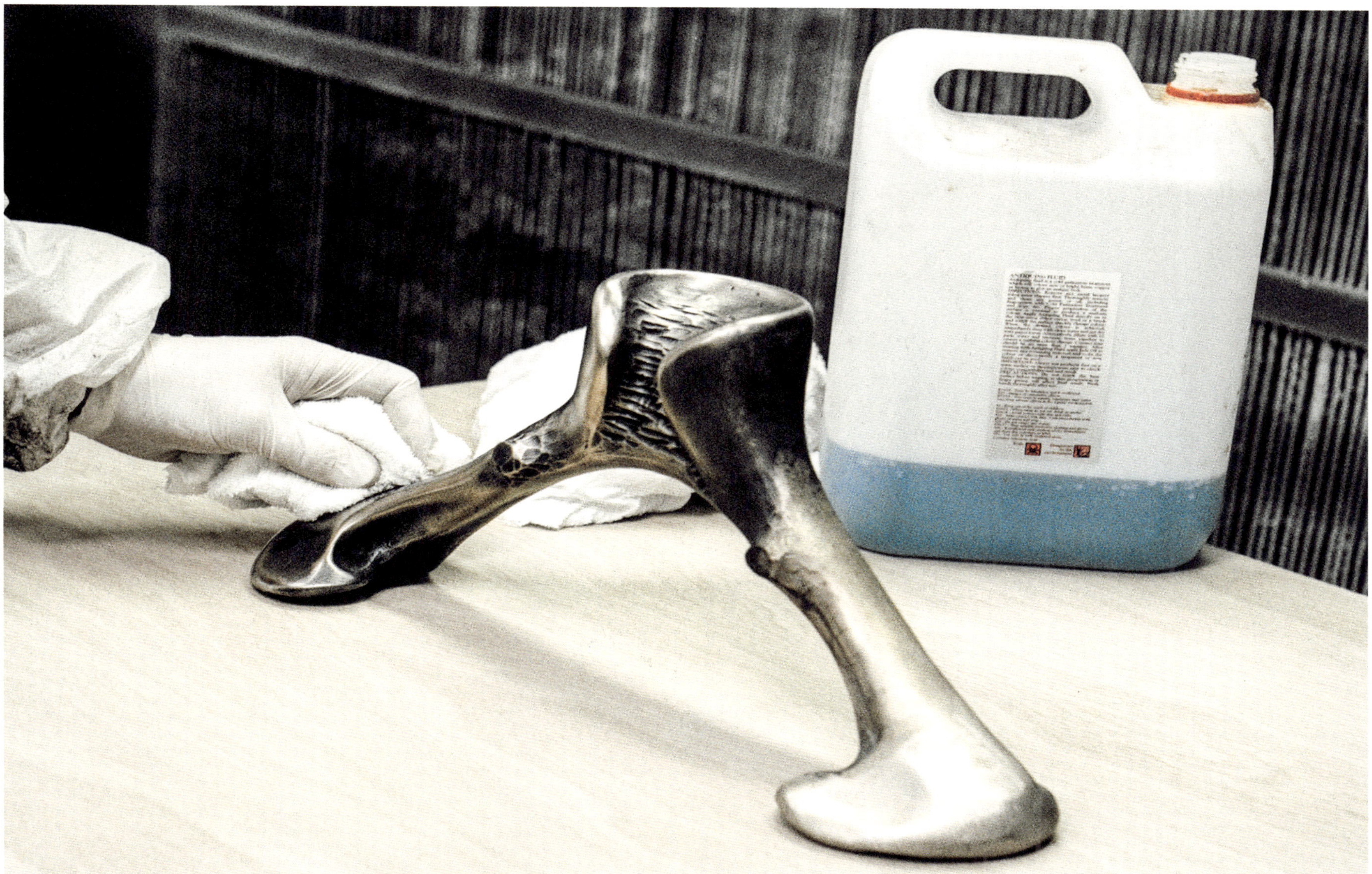

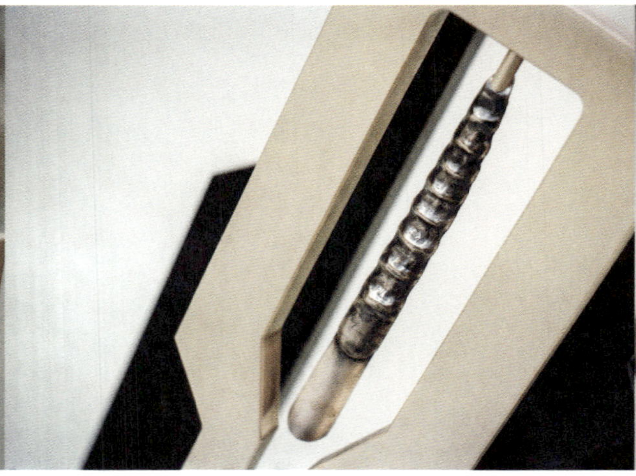

AURORA COFFEE TABLE

CITY CHEST OF DRAWERS

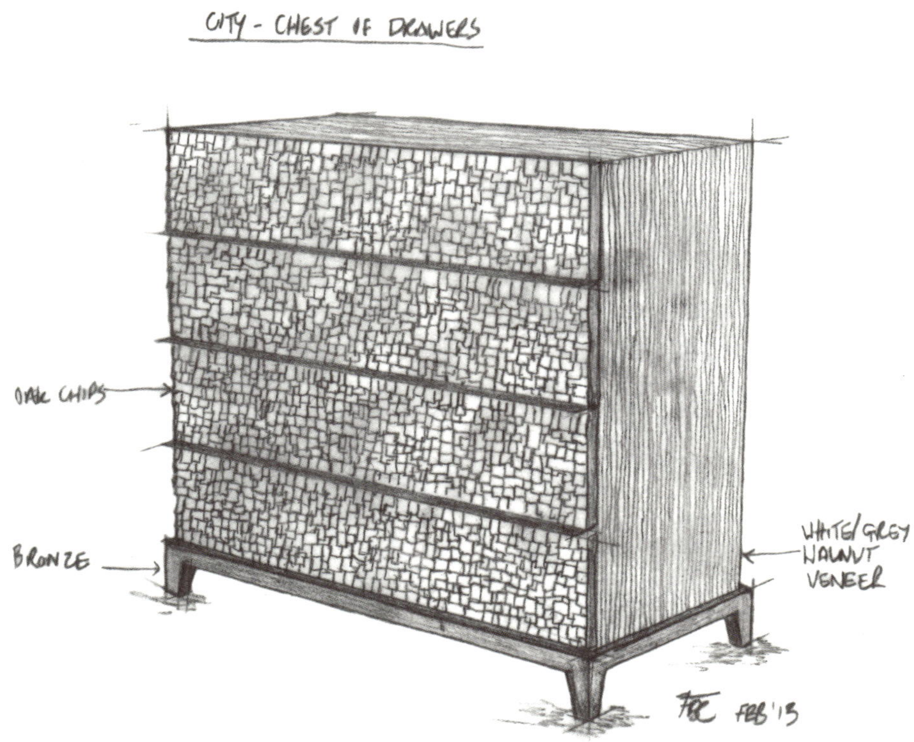

ACKNOWLEDGMENTS

The journey so far finally in print . . . how proud I am to see many years of work beautifully collated on these pages.

Every picture tells a story and that story is a true reflection of a collaborative effort from many skilled professionals. I would like to extend my greatest thanks to the following:

To my clients, for entrusting me to turn their vision into a reality. There is no greater satisfaction than waking up every day with the knowledge that you truly love what you do.

To my loyal and talented team, whose shared creativity, professionalism, and passion is displayed on a daily basis and who make each project a unique and enjoyable experience.

To the many contractors, for their patience with my pursuit of perfection and for understanding the constant evolution of design.

To the many artisans from all over the world, with whom we have had the pleasure of working and who have given us an educational insight into the fascinating processes of production.

To my husband, for his unconditional love and support at every step. And for the endless hours of enthusiastic discussions on business and design.

To our three wonderful children, who never fail to brighten my days with their innocence, love, and boundless energy.

To my wonderful parents, for giving me the opportunity to follow my dream into design, and to my siblings, for their unconditional support.

And finally to Charles and the whole team at Rizzoli . . . Thank you!

First published in the United States of America in 2019 by
Rizzoli International Publications, Inc.
300 Park Avenue South
New York, NY 10010
www.rizzoliusa.com

Publisher: Charles Miers
Designer: Fiona Barratt-Campbell, Sophie Callender, Samuele Belloni
Production Manager: Alyn Evans

Printed in Italy

2019 2020 2021 2022 2023 / 10 9 8 7 6 5 4 3 2 1

ISBN: 978–0–8478–6627–4
Library of Congress Control Number: 2019939829

Visit us online:
Facebook.com/RizzoliNewYork
Twitter: @Rizzoli_Books
Instagram.com/RizzoliBooks
Pinterest.com/RizzoliBooks
Youtube.com/user/RizzoliNY
Issuu.com/Rizzoli